BALTIMORE RAVENS

BY TOM GLAVE

The Child's World

Published by The Child's World®
1980 Lookout Drive • Mankato, MN 56003-1705
800-599-READ • www.childsworld.com

Acknowledgments
The Child's World®: Mary Berendes, Publishing Director
Red Line Editorial: Editorial direction
The Design Lab: Design
Amnet: Production

Design Element: Dean Bertoncelj/Shutterstock Images
Photographs ©: Aaron M. Sprecher/AP Images, cover, 1;
Nick Wass/AP Images 5, ; Wally Santana/AP Images 7, ;
Dave Hammond/AP Images 9, ; Gail Burton/AP Images 11, ;
Julia Robertson/AP Images 13, ; Mike Buscher/AP Images
14–15; Jeff Lewis/Icon Sportswire 17, ; Gene J. Puskar/AP
Images 19, ; Russell Tracy/Southcreek Global/Zuma Press/
Icon Sportswire 21, ; Jeff Lewis/Icon Sportswire 23, ; Zuma
Press/Icon Sportswire 25, ; Patrick Green/ Icon Sportswire
27, ; Carleton Hall/MMD/Icon Sportswire 29

ISBN 9781631439919
LCCN 2014959696

Printed in the United States of America
Mankato, MN
July, 2015
PA02265

ABOUT THE AUTHOR

Tom Glave grew up watching football on TV and playing it in the field next to his house. He learned to write about sports at the University of Missouri–Columbia and has written for newspapers in New Jersey, Missouri, Arkansas, and Texas. He lives near Houston, Texas, and cannot wait to play backyard football with his kids Tommy, Lucas, and Allison.

TABLE OF CONTENTS

GO, RAVENS!

Professional football left Baltimore in 1984. The Colts moved to Indianapolis that year. But Baltimore got a new team in 1996. The Cleveland Browns moved there. The team got a new name and colors. The Baltimore Ravens were born. The Ravens won the **Super Bowl** in their fifth year. They added another title after the 2012 season. Baltimore is known for its strong defense. Let's meet the Ravens.

Baltimore finished in the top six in points allowed per game in 11 of its first 19 seasons.

WHO ARE THE RAVENS?

The Baltimore Ravens play in the National Football **League** (NFL). They are one of the 32 teams in the NFL. The NFL includes the American Football Conference (AFC) and the National Football Conference (NFC). The winner of the AFC plays the winner of the NFC in the Super Bowl. The Ravens play in the North Division of the AFC. The Ravens have been very successful. They had only six losing years in their first 19 seasons.

Offensive tackle Jonathan Ogden, Baltimore's first draft pick, was inducted into the Pro Football Hall of Fame in 2013.

WHERE THEY CAME FROM

Baltimore had the Colts from 1953 to 1983. But the team owner moved them to Indianapolis. Fans were upset. Art Modell owned the Cleveland Browns. He wanted a new stadium for his team. He could not get one in Cleveland. So Modell moved the Browns to Baltimore after the 1995 season. The team got a new stadium there. The NFL let Modell keep his players. But Cleveland kept the Browns name and history. The new Baltimore team needed a name. Fans chose "The Ravens." It came from Edgar Allen Poe's poem "The Raven." Poe was from Baltimore.

Quarterback Vinny Testaverde celebrates with fans after scoring the first touchdown in Ravens history on September 1, 1996.

WHO THEY PLAY

The Baltimore Ravens play 16 games each season. With so few games, each one is important. Every year, the Ravens play two games against each of the other three teams in their division. Those teams are the Cleveland Browns, Pittsburgh Steelers, and Cincinnati Bengals. The Ravens also play six other teams from the AFC and four from the NFC. The Ravens and Steelers have a hard-hitting **rivalry**. It is one of the best in the NFL. Both teams usually have tough defenses. The Browns are another rival because of the teams' shared history.

Games between the Ravens and Steelers are often defensive slugfests full of hard hits.

WHERE THEY PLAY

The Colts played in Memorial Stadium while in Baltimore. The Ravens also played there for two years. Now they play in M&T Bank Stadium. It opened in 1998. It holds 71,008 fans. There are statues of Colts quarterback Johnny Unitas and Ravens linebacker Ray Lewis outside the building. M&T Bank Stadium also hosts other sporting events and concerts.

The same architects that designed M&T Bank Stadium also designed Oriole Park at Camden Yards, home of the Baltimore Orioles baseball team.

THE FOOTBALL FIELD

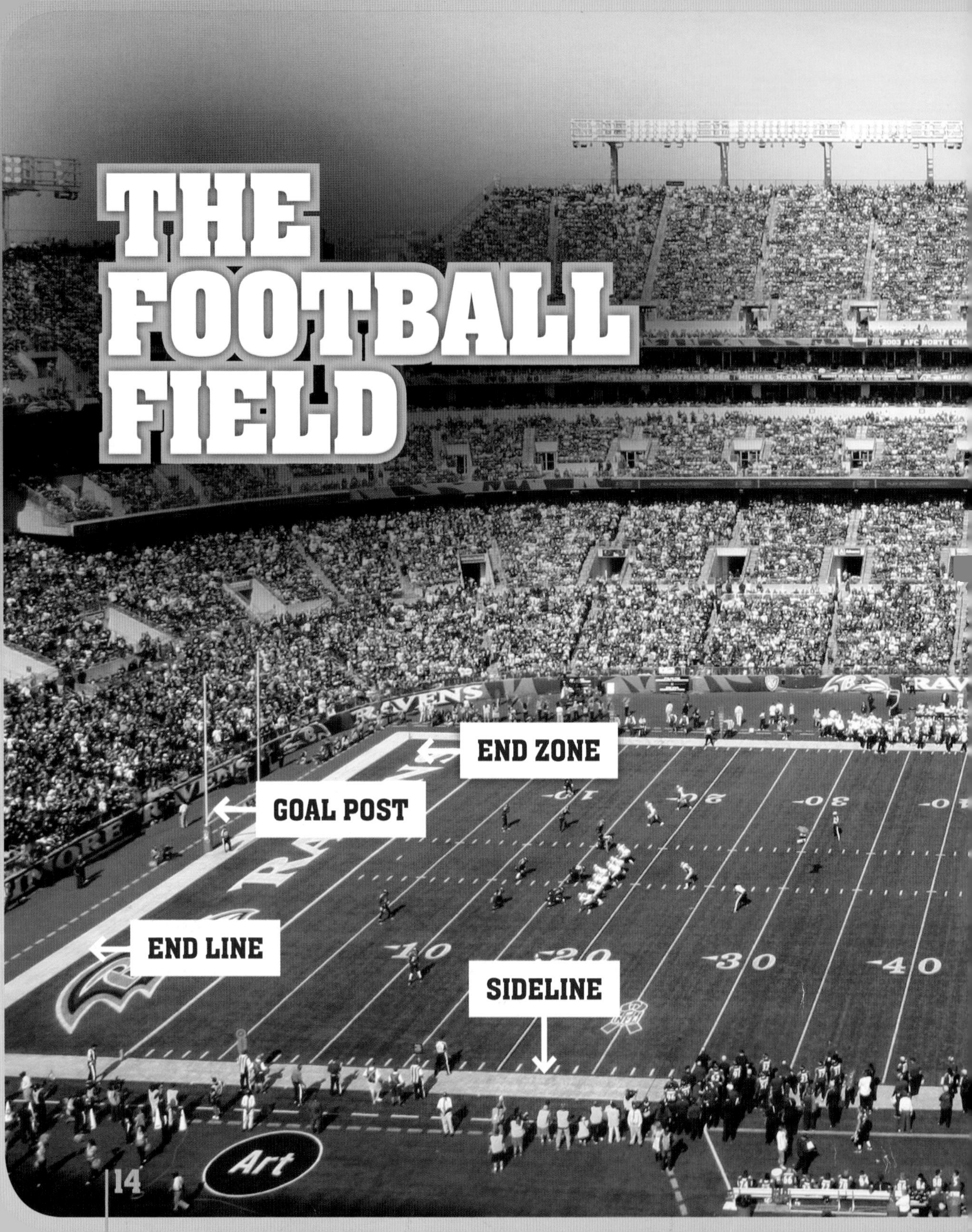

END ZONE

GOAL POST

END LINE

SIDELINE

HASH MARKS

MIDFIELD

20-YARD LINE

GOAL LINE →

BENCH AREA

BIG DAYS

The Ravens have had some great moments in their history. Here are three of the greatest:

2000—Baltimore's defense was incredible. It allowed just 165 points all regular season. That was an NFL record for a 16-game season. The great play continued in the **playoffs**. The Ravens played four games. They allowed only 23 total points. That included a 34-7 Super Bowl win.

2003—It was September 14. The Ravens were playing the Cleveland Browns. Running back Jamal Lewis went wild. He rushed for 295 yards. That was an NFL record until 2007. He finished the season with 2,066 rushing yards. That was second-most ever at the time. Baltimore won its first AFC North title that year.

Safety Ed Reed celebrates after the Ravens beat the San Francisco 49ers in the Super Bowl on February 3, 2013.

2013—The 2012 Ravens were playoff **underdogs**. But quarterback Joe Flacco took over. He threw 11 **touchdown** passes and no interceptions in four games. That included the Super Bowl. Baltimore beat the San Francisco 49ers 34–31 on February 3. There was a blackout in the second half. The stadium lights went out for 34 minutes. But even that did not stop Baltimore.

TOUGH DAYS

Football is a hard game. Even the best teams have rough games and seasons. Here are some of the toughest times in Ravens history:

1996—It was the Ravens' first season. Fans were excited to have NFL football back in Baltimore. But the team was bad. It went 4-12. That is still the Ravens' worst record through 2014.

2009—The 2008 Ravens made the AFC title game. They played the Pittsburgh Steelers on January 18. The winner would go to the Super Bowl. Pittsburgh won 23-14. Through the 2014 season, the Ravens were 1-3 against the Steelers in the playoffs.

Pittsburgh safety Troy Polamalu (43) sacks Baltimore quarterback Joe Flacco (5) in the Ravens' 23-14 AFC Championship Game loss to the rival Steelers on January 18, 2009.

2013—Linebacker Ray Lewis retired before the season. He had been the team leader. The Ravens were fighting for the playoffs. They had to win their final game. But they lost. Baltimore missed the postseason for the first time since 2007.

MEET THE FANS

Baltimore fans wear purple on Fridays before home games. It is one of the team's colors. The team mascot is Poe. It is a black raven. Poe wears a Ravens uniform. Two live ravens are on the sidelines for home games. They are named Rise and Conquer. They live at the Maryland Zoo. The Marching Ravens are a marching band that led victory parades after the team's Super Bowl wins.

Baltimore's mascot is named after famous poet Edgar Allen Poe, who also inspired the team's name.

HEROES THEN

Running back Jamal Lewis ran for 1,364 yards in 2000. That was a Ravens **rookie** record. Lewis led the NFL with 2,066 rushing yards in 2003. Offensive tackle Jonathan Ogden is in the Pro Football Hall of Fame. He was a strong blocker. Linebacker Ray Lewis was an emotional leader. He played for 17 years. He was the NFL Defensive Player of the Year in 2000 and 2003. He was also the **Most Valuable Player (MVP)** of the Ravens' first Super Bowl win. Safety Ed Reed played 11 seasons with Baltimore. He led the NFL in interceptions three times in that span.

Linebacker Ray Lewis was famous for doing a dance before games to get Ravens fans pumped up.

HEROES NOW

Quarterback Joe Flacco joined the Ravens in 2008. He led Baltimore to the playoffs in each of his first five seasons. No other NFL quarterback had done that. He was the MVP of Baltimore's second Super Bowl win. Linebackers Terrell Suggs and C. J. Mosley keep Baltimore's defensive tradition strong. Suggs had 14 sacks in 2011. He was named NFL Defensive Player of the Year. Defensive end Elvis Dumervil had 17 sacks in 2014.

Linebacker Terrell Suggs is just the latest in a long line of great Ravens defenders.

GEARING UP

NFL players wear team uniforms. They wear helmets and pads to keep them safe. Cleats help them make quick moves and run fast. Some players wear extra gear for protection.

THE FOOTBALL

NFL footballs are made of leather. Under the leather is a lining that fills with air to give the ball its shape. The leather has bumps or "pebbles." These help players grip the ball. Laces help players control their throws. Footballs are also called "pigskins" because some of the first balls were made from pig bladders. Today they are made of leather from cows.

Defensive tackle Haloti Ngata made five Pro Bowls during his nine seasons with the Ravens.

HELMET

SHOULDER PADS

GLOVES

FOOTBALL

CLEATS

SPORTS STATS

 Here are some of the all-time career records for the Baltimore Ravens. All the stats are through the 2014 season.

RUSHING YARDS

Jamal Lewis 7,801

Ray Rice 6,180

RECEPTIONS

Derrick Mason 471

Todd Heap 467

PASSING YARDS

Joe Flacco 25,531

Kyle Boller 7,846

INTERCEPTIONS

Ed Reed 61

Ray Lewis 31

SACKS

Terrell Suggs 106.5

Peter Boulware 70

POINTS

Matt Stover 1,464

Justin Tucker 401

Running back Jamal Lewis's historic 2003 season earned him a Pro Bowl appearance.

TOTAL TOUCHDOWNS

Jamal Lewis 47

Ray Rice 43

GLOSSARY

league an organization of sports teams that compete against each other

Most Valuable Player (MVP) a yearly award given to the top player in the NFL

playoffs a series of games after the regular season that decides which two teams play in the Super Bowl

rivalry an ongoing competition between teams that play each other often, over a long time

rookie a player playing in his first season

Super Bowl the championship game of the NFL, played between the winners of the AFC and the NFC

touchdown a play in which the ball is held in the other team's end zone, resulting in six points

underdogs teams that are not expected to win

FIND OUT MORE

IN THE LIBRARY

Frisch, Aaron. *Baltimore Ravens*. Madison,
WI: Creative Paperbacks, 2014.

Gigliotti, Jim. *Super Bowl Super Teams*.
New York: Scholastic, 2010.

Nagelhout, Ryan. *Joe Flacco*.
New York: Gareth Stevens Publishing, 2014.

ON THE WEB

Visit our Web site for links about the Baltimore Ravens:
childsworld.com/links

*Note to Parents, Teachers, and Librarians: We routinely verify our Web links to make
sure they are safe and active sites. So encourage your readers to check them out!*

INDEX